FOOTBALL AND THE WILL

FOOTBALL AND THE WILL

How to Create the Perfect Team

Steve Dickson

2016

First published in Great Britain in 2016 by Adam & Eve Books

Cover photo of Gordon Smith © Herald & Times Group
Cover design and layout by Antonia Becht

ISBN 978-0-9935868-0-4

In memory of Robert Riddell Dickson (1929–1995)

Author's Note

The objective of this short work is to use philosophy to explore the relationship between brilliant play and the 'religious' dimension of the beautiful game called football, and to map out a path to the unified will which we need to create a truly great team. It contains a novel way of combining Heidegger's *authenticity* and Schopenhauer's *will* with the idea of *ritual*. It in no way represents any orthodox school of Heidegger studies.

Many thanks to Jonathan Wilson whose excellent book *Inverting the Pyramid: The History of Football Tactics* opened the door to the numerous examples which illustrate the theory advocated here.

CONTENTS

Football is the last sacred ritual of our time.

Pier Paolo Pasolini

PROLOGUE

Like many children, I grew up in a home with a father obsessed. At the beginning of the 1950s something profound had been revealed to him on a regular basis, every second Saturday at Easter Road. From the stories of what he witnessed, I imagined the ball levitating magically above the head and superhuman limbs of Gordon Smith, on the right wing of the five attackers, *The Famous Five,* as again and again they swept towards their opponents' goal.

Though possibly an anachronism even then, their 2–3–5 formation was immensely successful. In a six-year period between 1948 and 1953, Hibernian won the championship three times and lost another two by the narrowest of margins. Each of their five attackers scored more than 100 goals for the club.

As a teenager, I put my father's obsession down to nostalgia for a golden age, ancient history, irrelevant to my own world of Pink Floyd and flared jeans. But that remarkable team resonates still, and rather than consigning it to the realm of myth and legend, perhaps we can seek to discover and resurrect something of its essence, so that it may again live on in the game we all love.

INTRODUCTION

... the Spurs principle is to hold the ball a minimum amount of time, keep it on the ground and put it ahead into an open space where a colleague will be a second or two later. The result is their attacks are carried on right through the side with each man taking the ball in his stride at top pace, for all the world like a wave gathering momentum as it races to the far distant shore. It is all worked out in triangles and squares and when the mechanism of it clicks at speed ... there is simply no defence against it.

Daily Telegraph, November 1950[1]

What makes a football team great? Is there a single crucial factor? An easier question might be: what do great teams have in common? For example, Brazil of 1970; Barcelona; Bayern Munich; Ajax at their peak; Hungary in the 1950s and many others all share something momentous.

Two things specifically spring to mind. First, they inspire in their audience a sense of profound meaning, as if the creative flow of their attacking play has been touched by the gods. Their play manifests a certain kind of beauty, one that brings us nearer to the very soul of football itself. Not surprisingly these teams inspire loyalty, passion, excitement, even love. Secondly, great teams give the appearance of playing with a single 'will', as if the team becomes a single 'being' in which its players have a telepathic connection and its collective actions transcend the sum of its individual talents.

Could it be that these two things are interrelated? Perhaps there is some connection between the audience reaction and the *being* of the team, that the audience can experience, or share that *being*, in some elemental way. If we can understand what makes a team great, then we have a better chance of creating such a team, not by accident, or through the determination of a unique and extraordinary coach, but consciously and deliberately, step by step. Perhaps a bit of philosophy can help us.

The German philosopher Martin Heidegger had a concept called *Authenticity*.[2] This is a state of *being*, arising, for example, from the skilled performance of a practical ability. It results in a kind of mystical unity: boundaries between doer and doing, tool and world, all become fluid and begin to break down; everything appears interconnected. One aspect of this state is the absence of thought. It is pure doing, pure *will.* It is intuitive and spontaneous, but it also has a mystical, quasi-religious dimension. This idea will help us explain why great football teams in action generate a sense of revelation in the spectator.

We might imagine that great teams think, not as a collection of individuals, but as a single team. However, I would suggest that they do not think at all, they simply act. The understanding, strategy, tactics are somehow in the will itself; in the play itself. These must happen spontaneously, intuitively; there is no time for deliberation.

There can be individual 'beings' or collective 'beings', but the key to understanding what a being is lies in the repeated structures of its action, of its will. These repeated structures we can call 'rituals'. So, if a team is to be a single collective 'being' it must perform certain types of collective rituals. The more intensively these rituals are performed, then the more coherent the team 'being', and the team 'will', will become.

If a team wants to adopt a fast, attacking approach to the game, then those dynamic principles must be embodied in the rituals it performs. That attacking logic then becomes central to the fabric of the team, to its very *being*; it is manifest in the structure of its will. These attacking rituals and drills, then, must become absolutely central to that team's training programme, alongside the usual fitness, ball skills, etc.

The focus of team *will* can also be increased by eliminating those elements which might disrupt it, such as individual egos, psychological habits of resentment, individual ambition, claims of unfair treatment by the referee, cynical play, diving, and so on. All of these things disrupt the collective or 'transcendent' will of the team, and undermine the beauty and ethos of the game. In Heidegger's terms they would be called 'inauthentic', because they strengthen divisions between players, and between players and the game, and so negate the mystical unity associated with skilled performance. Thus, great play, positive values, and the team *being* are all bound up together.

A coordinated team *will* is important not just for attack, but also for defence and the transitions between the two. *Pressing*, which has become so important to the modern game, is so much more effective and efficient if orchestrated rather than piecemeal: a tactic used by Barcelona to great effect over the years.

Great teams are usually associated with single-minded coaches: those with vision, strict discipline, rigorous training regimes and tactical innovations. Also, the process of a team becoming a coherent *being* is, to some extent, a naturally occurring one when a group of players play together over extended periods. However, understanding the principles at work here reduces the element of chance, reliance on luck, and the need for an extraordinary coach. It significantly improves the practical prospect of creating a great team, given that the necessary training structures are put in place.

Successful coaches have sometimes been ready to use ideas borrowed from other disciplines to enhance their methods. Here, the main emphasis is on philosophy (Heidegger's *Authenticity* and Schopenhauer's *Will*),[3] but other belief systems and disciplines can also be useful, such as Zen Buddhism, martial arts, Roman military tactics, etc. If borrowed ideas take us closer to our goal of great football, then we should not be afraid of people's reactions: genuine fans will be loyal (and understanding) to their team, regardless of their methods, if they are true to the spirit of the game and play the kind of football that quickens the pulse.

I make no apology for basing this argument on a value judgment. I will argue that dynamic, attacking play is the essence of the game, and that it is precisely this dimension which must be central to the team's *being*. Only through the dynamic exercise of its collective *will* can the imagination, creativity and innovation of individual players become fully realized, and so inspire what we seek most from the game: wonder and a sense of the incredible.

1
THINKING VERSUS DOING

In a way he had brains in his legs, and many remarkable things occurred to them while they were running.

Alfred Polgar[4] on Matthias Sindelar, Austria's greatest player.

A team playing well has no time to deliberate; its reactions are lightning fast, its attack spontaneous. If a player starts to think, the result is fatal. We have all seen those films showing thousands of small fish swimming as one, twisting and turning in perfect unison. Those individual fish don't think, they don't communicate with each other; rather they act as a single being, with a single will.

For both individuals and teams, thinking is slow, linear, and can only be directed towards one thing at a time. *Doing*, on the other hand, is multifaceted. We can perform multiple tasks simultaneously, but only if we are completely in the moment, fully present and not distracted by thought.

Thinking is useless for great play, and there is no time for communicating. We can't think about what we're doing while dancing or playing music, we must 'feel'. We must intuit the form of the discipline and the performance of the other dancers or players.

One of the most intriguing, and undeniable, properties of great athletic performance lies in the impossibility of regulating certain central skills by overt mental deliberation; the required action simply doesn't grant sufficient time for the sequential processing of conscious decisions.

Stephen Jay Gould [5]

In martial arts, the swordsman, for example, seeks the Zen state of *mushin,* or *no-mind*, and so becomes one with the sword, moving intuitively, creatively, instantly; performance and complete focus of being go hand in hand. Likewise, the footballer must aim to be at one with the ball, with the positions of their teammates, the spaces between them, with the opposing players, and with their team's strategy and tactics.

We talk of an athlete being 'in the zone'. *This is not a psychological state, but a state of being.* If a player begins to think on the pitch then their whole multidimensional skill set evaporates and the magical flow of play is lost.

In philosophy, the question 'what is being?' is fundamental. Answers traditionally take the form of listing a thing's attributes, or trying to define its essence. The standard model of human *being*, the legacy of René Descartes (1596–1650) is that we are first of all thinking things, minds forever marooned in our physical bodies – the two things quite distinct. Heidegger took a totally different approach and proposed instead that a thing's *being* depends on *how* it exists in the world; the *way* in which it exists in the world. Therefore, time becomes an essential element in its being. So now, mind and body are just two aspects of the same thing, the gulf between them has gone.

As I understand Heidegger (and he's not so easy to understand), what's important to a being, then, are the repeated structures of its *doing*, of its action in the world. The doing itself I call *will*, and the structures *rituals*. Seeing Schopenhauer's theory of *Will* in this new light reveals the world in a new way.

But to be clear: will is not the same thing as desire or intention, but simply 'doing'. If a ball is thrown at me I don't have to think: *a ball is approaching, I'd better raise my hands.* I just react immediately; I catch it or knock it aside intuitively. A newborn child doesn't have to learn how to cry or move its limbs. It appears in the world with will already flowing in its being. Will is its *mode* of being. Through time it learns to orientate to that will, but the will is the very ground or basis of its being.

An individual is characterized by the rituals he or she performs. We can see, for example, how addictive rituals quickly change an individual. Repeated rituals have their associated values: for instance, religious rituals have their associated beliefs and faiths.

Similarly, a team's being is defined by how it acts in the world, the repeated structures of its play, its training, and all the other team activities, such as travel, eating together, etc. The values by which a team lives and plays are completely bound up with these repeated structures.

To explain the concept of Authenticity, Heidegger uses the example of an artisan hammering. As he hammers successfully, skilfully, in full flow, the boundaries between man and hammer, and between man and world, begin to drop away, and there emerges a kind of unity, or interconnectedness. This could be described as similar in nature to the mystical unity of certain religions.[6] A further result of this unity is the sense of revelation of meaning, both to the performer and to any spectators present.

This meaning cannot be described verbally, it transcends language, but we could say that it results from the action of 'transcendent' will, freed from individual ego, and which unifies all. The performance, or act of will, is a fully committed 'doing', but one which has a certain detachment, as it is not *owned* by any particular ego. So it is a doing, but also a non-doing, which, incidentally, sounds rather like Taoism, with its associated aim of being at one with the Tao. (There is some evidence that Heidegger, like Schopenhauer, was deeply influenced by Eastern philosophy.)[7]

A team also aims for this state of authenticity: a collective 'no-mind', where every player is completely present and at one with the flow and rhythm of the game. Since the boundaries between players have begun to drop away and each feels this state of interconnectedness, their ability to play as a unified team with a single will can become a reality.

Authenticity also means a heightened sensitivity to the kinetic properties of the ball. The momentum of the ball and its movement in the flow of play is determined by those kinetic properties. The ideal team has an intuitive *feel* for this momentum. The material nature of the ball and the team's *being* are inseparable aspects of play.

Will is not something that acts *on* the world. It is *in* the world, it is part of the physical world. Will and the physical properties of the world (like the weight and shape of a football) are aspects of each other. The will of all living things has evolved and developed in, and through, the properties of the physical universe since the beginnings of life on Earth, so the two are indivisible. This means we can say will is 'in' the world. Will cannot exist in any sense outside the physical world.

Will and the physical world are perfectly balanced, so skilled performance of a practical ability is, in an elemental way, a fulfilment of the world. It is a natural harmony. But that harmony must not be disrupted, it must be allowed to *sing*. When Barcelona attack the opponent's goal at speed, this harmony is allowed to sing most clearly. So excellent performance requires an intuitive, uninterrupted flow of will. In this state of authenticity, we can describe that will as transcendent.

A football is a human artefact. It is a product of, and encapsulates, the culture of the game. It already contains within itself all the things that can be done with it in play. To find transcendent will *in* the ball means that team and ball can share that will; are unified with it in a profound way.

The team, in this state of authenticity, animated as it is by transcendent will, inevitably has transcendent values. Ego and self-interest are not compatible with this state of authenticity. Cheating and cynical tactics not only demean the human spirit but completely undermine the mysterious flow and balance of the authentic state. Positive or unselfish values, then, are not only a question of morality, but also play a fundamental role in the mechanics of skilled team performance.

Thought, of course, is vital off the pitch, in planning and strategy, but explanations and verbal instructions are completely forgotten in the pressure and chaos of play, where the team will revert to instinct. We must give form to that team's collective instinct through training rituals so that in the heat of battle it will spontaneously perform the right techniques and tactical manoeuvres.

Football happens in the physical world, in the same space–time where human *being* dwells. In skilled performance, *doing* and *being* and *play* are all inseparable parts of the one enigmatic whole. In this authentic state of optimal performance, Being and Time become one and the same. But thought drives a wedge between them. Thought undermines this fragile unity. It disrupts the possibility of great play and so must be sidelined. Remove thought and our experience of both Being and Time changes. All is then unified by will, including the members of a team, so we can enter a world where football becomes poetry.

2
THE ATTACK: A FORWARD DYNAMIC

Kreisel could be described as ... a one-touch, very quick, short and ground passing game ... the team-mates used to maneuver into spaces all over the pitch ... and it is these favourable positions ... that determine where the next pass will be directed ... This way there appeared to be a telepathic communication between the passer and the intended receiver, a communication the oppositions were never able to intercept, making them dizzy ... thus the name – Spinning Top. Schalke's game was all about passing, movement off the ball to find an unmarked position to receive possession ...

Arnav Bose [8]

The whole line of forwards is on the run together. Until it loses the ball or shoots at goal, it does not stop ...

C. B. Fry on Corinthians, 1890s.

Being has its own built-in momentum; that is its nature. It is the pattern of will across time: every living thing is constantly 'doing'. But transcendent will, which is the momentum of being, is not a force like electricity or gravity which animates things, but simply the *way* they jointly exist in the world. We can let this momentum pass through us or we can engage with it, like surfing a wave. Similarly, a team can orientate itself with that momentum, so that its mode of being can be a constantly forward-moving dynamic.

To achieve this, we need to have some sense of the attacking structure, understand how that structure can become central to the *being* of the team, and then devise a practical means to make that a concrete reality.

The most important thing in football is what a player is doing on a pitch when he's not in possession of the ball, not when he has it.

Valeriy Lobanovskyi [9]

The triangular attacking structure, where the ball is played into space and simultaneously a man off the ball runs into that space to meet it, is fundamental to the game. Done well, as part of an attack, and especially when leading to a goal, it is a thing of beauty, but it cannot be performed through thinking or communication. The process must be spontaneous, intuitive, completely without hesitation. The players involved must have a shared knowledge of what is required, one that is completely internalized and manifest solely in action: they must have a shared will. The result is the appearance of telepathic communication.

Leicester's counterattack has been even more effective and incisive than usual ... The Leicester XI, having played together more minutes than any other group in the Premier League, seem almost telepathic in their ability to recognise each other's runs in transition. This familiarity has made Leicester the most dangerous team in the open field.

Michael Caley [10]

Roman soldiers trained and drilled endlessly so they would become a single fighting unit, with mutual trust and respect, and pride in the collective performance. Working in teams, one team would probe the defence of the enemy soldiers, provoking a defensive reaction that would leave those enemy soldiers exposed in another area. That weakness would instantly be exploited by another Roman team moving forward. Or, on command, the frontline soldiers facing their enemy would stab diagonally behind the defence of the enemy soldier to his left. In doing so, the Roman left himself open to attack from the enemy soldier facing him, so he needed to trust his colleague to his right to perform the same move at exactly the same moment. In effect, he was part of the collective being: his survival, and that of the group, one and the same.

On the pitch, the aims are similar: to collectively probe and create imbalance in the enemy defence; and, together, to recognize that weakness and exploit it. But this can only work with total trust in the team structure.

... as soon as there is the possibility of exploiting imbalance the ball should be played forwards. Play the ball into space, into the back room (the area behind the opponent's defence) very quickly, with few touches of the ball and with lots of movement off it.

Egil Olsen [11]

In *possession football* the majority of passes between teammates in a game are made when players are either stationary or moving slowly, with the ball played directly from one to the other. However, in a fast attack, the ball is played into empty space on the run. These are two quite different modes, the second with an extra dimension whereby the three-dimensional frame of reference of the first mode is itself now moving forward.

This fourth dimension is the crucial element in great play and exactly what we want to place at the centre of the team's being, to become central to what the team 'is'. It means that the team's *being* stretches out across time, and is the *way* the attacking team exists in the world. But its being also exists in relation to space, particularly that open space between the opposing defenders and their goal – the 'back room'. The team's being always seeks to penetrate this space, to cross it with speed towards the goal. It draws the attackers like the implacable pull of gravity.

Teams for which possession football has become central to their way of being often have difficulty making the leap to that forward-moving, attacking frame of reference. They become too complacent and comfortable retaining the ball, so that the leap to attack requires deliberate communication and finding extra psychological motivation, rather than being spontaneous and instinctive.

Charles Reep (1904–2002) has been credited with establishing the dominance of the *long ball game* in English football. In the 1950s he produced statistical data which purported to show that the vast majority of goals came from short attacks of three passes or less. However, with statistics we can prove or disprove almost anything depending on the frame of reference we choose, how we define the parameters, and the variables we include or ignore.

In the end Reep simply wanted to use statistical analysis to promote the kind of attacking football he preferred. His point was that the more attacks on goal your team can make within the 90 minutes of play, the more goals they will score. The quicker you get to goal, with the fewest passes, then the more attacks you can complete and the higher the goal conversion.

It's not about the long ball or the short ball, it's about the right ball.

Bob Paisley

At the time, the implications of Reep's analysis seem to have been misunderstood (perhaps even by himself). It does not follow that the *long ball game* or the *kick and rush* approach is the best method for success. Three accurate through passes into space with players on the run to intercept can cover huge distances very quickly. Fast attacking play requires passing accuracy and creativity, not a gung-ho, *get the ball up the park* kind of mentality.

The 'reacher' and the 'through pass' might look similar, and may be conflated in the statistical record, but there is a world of difference between an optimistic long ball and an accurate long pass into space to the exact place where a teammate will shortly arrive. However, the basic point of Reep's attacking approach still stands.

Graham Taylor's phenomenal success at Watford, gaining four promotions in five seasons, is only partly due to the influence of Reep's philosophy. Taylor was also influenced by Victor Maslov's aggressive pressing game, and it is this, beautifully combined with the fast attack, which largely accounts for Watford's amazing feat in the English league. Watford's failure in Europe is often used by critics of Reep as an example of the limits of his approach. But this is unfair since success or failure is never due to a single factor or element but always a result of many things.

*

In the attacking movement, a pass into space where a running teammate will shortly be, is a projection not just across space but also across time, it is a projection into the future. The objective must be to make this *way* of being, completely natural for the team, so its instinct is to act in such a way. It is not the case that the team must think in this way; rather, it must intuitively and automatically *play* in this way, this logic must become the team's being. It must *inhabit* that forward-moving dimension.

Thinking is totally alien to this kind of intuitive performance. Thinking is locked in a temporal dimension, whereas intuitive performance transcends time. Authentic being (the state of optimal performance) is stretched out across time. It does not pass through time but rather time lies within the structure of its being, so that fast attacking play is simply the unfolding of its being.

We sometimes have a sense of being outside historical time, e.g. when listening to music in a particular moment or place, or in the performance of a religious or meaningful ritual. Time has 'stopped', we have entered 'sacred' time where we are open to a sense of destiny, where we occupy an 'epic' frame of reference and where the world and our place within it have undergone some dramatic transformation. This phenomenon is elemental in the generation of human meaning, and explains why a sport such as football embodies a religious dimension for so many.

If we are successful in constructing such an attacking team, then the forward momentum becomes the team's default mode, and the team's state of equilibrium incorporates this dynamic force. On the pitch, without this forward momentum, the team is not in equilibrium so, like the addict suffering 'cold turkey', whose only objective is to re-establish equilibrium through the addictive agent, the team wants to re-establish this attacking way of being. Without the forward-moving dynamic, the team is in crisis mode: its sense of identity requires it.

Crucially, this would mean that there is never a problem with lack of psychological motivation. The motivation is self-contained in the very being of the team. At each point, the team is oriented towards the next stage of the attack. *The development of the attack is its purpose for being.*

We must adopt this forward-moving frame of reference, because it places the attacking dynamic at the absolute centre of the team's way of being. So that way is hard-wired, central to what they are. Creative, self-disciplined, yet spontaneous attack can always outwit a dogged defence. A two-man attacking combination pass, in the form of a fast intuitive one-two, can slice through the tightest defence, chop-chop. The three-man move is even more dangerous when it is like music and poetry, completely uninhibited by thought.

Three games which clearly illustrate this principle are: Celtic's victory over Internazionale in the 1967 European Cup; Brazil's victory over Italy in the 1970 World Cup final; and Ajax's win against Internazionale in the 1972 European Cup. In each case the winning team broke down the locked defence (the *Catenaccio*) of the Italian teams. And in each case the winning team made an absolute commitment to forward-moving attacking play.

Jock Stein said before the 1967 game: '… we are going to attack as we have never attacked before.' And: 'Cups are not won by individuals. They are won by men in a team, men who put their club before personal prestige. I am lucky – I have the players who do just that for Celtic.'

Interestingly, the Dutch system of Total Football, where players can switch positions, is at work not just in the Ajax game, but there are aspects of it also in the other two games. In both, highly mobile defenders joined the attacks and scored. (*Total Football* – see Chapter 5.) It is no surprise, then, that it is these kind of teams, with their total commitment and authenticity, which inspire the most intense feelings and leave the most indelible memories.

But how are we to create such a team? Beings, both individual and collective, are, as we have said, characterized by the repeated structures of their will, their rituals. They are also shaped and moulded by those rituals, and any new rituals which are performed repeatedly. So the way to change, or form, the being of a team, lies in ritualizing particular structures of training.

The most obvious strategy here is for the team's coach to devise training drills where only passing into space on the run is permitted, and passing directly to other teammates is forbidden. Only by the endless, constant and intense performance of this training ritual can the forward-moving dynamic eventually become central to how the team exists in the world: its *way* of being. This does not mean, of course, that other drills and methods of training must be dropped. It means simply that the attacking ritual must always have absolute priority.

Finally, when these attacking movements become second nature to the team, when they can be performed spontaneously by all, then spectacular play becomes possible. Creative innovation follows naturally from this spontaneity, and is the final step in the development of team being. This is the point where the rules of the game come fully to life; are made manifest; where the game can be played in that extraordinary mode (which we have called the state of authenticity), where it inspires awe and a palpable state of joy in the fans. It is then, truly, the beautiful game.

3
INDIVIDUAL CREATIVITY

I didn't want solo artists; I wanted an orchestra. The greatest compliment I received was when people said my football was like music.

Arrigo Sacchi, legendary coach of AC Milan.

The relationship between individual and team is a complex one, and extremely important. Once the team has internalized the attacking structures, then individual talent can be expressed through the team dynamic, as a part of the team being.

Competitiveness between players is also transformed into joint creative endeavour within the team structure. The alchemy of the Lennon–McCartney relationship, for example, was only possible within the structure of the Beatles. Remove that structure and the genius is dissipated, the creative dynamic lost. Within the team structure, indivi–

dual talent is elevated to a new dimension. Cut from its ties to individual ego, it undergoes a dramatic transformation.

Recently I witnessed a group of Germans being taught a Scottish country dance. The exact details of the dance are not important, but roughly speaking the dance was as follows: perhaps thirty couples were arranged in a circle around the hall. Each couple, standing side by side, their arms linked behind and in front, takes three strides forward, pivots, and then takes three steps backwards. The woman turns under the man's raised arm, each couple does a short polka round and round, advancing the circle of dancers, then the woman breaks off to join the male of the couple behind and the whole thing is repeated.

At the beginning there was total chaos. Confusion reigned. The dancers were awkward, self-conscious, embarrassed. Couples crashed into each other, so the circle of dancers did not rotate smoothly but alternately stretched and bunched up. I could see the dancers think to themselves, 'Is this the way to do it?' They talked to each other, giving each other advice and guidance, or argued about what was correct. At each change several dancers were left without partners and had to run around to search for the nearest free male or female. Some dancers appeared to understand fairly quickly, others looked hopeless.

However, as the minutes passed something extraordinary began to happen: the collective dance seemed to find itself as more and more dancers got the knack. This was not an intellectual understanding but a means of acquiring a bodily ability to 'do' in terms of space, rhythm and timing. As this ability became internalised and automatic for each dancer, they each got an increasing *feel* for what the whole group was doing, a whole-group awareness. Their individual actions became orientated towards the group. Before long they acted with a collective single will. The circle of dancers now moved smoothly, flowed naturally as one. Something quite profound had happened.

To my surprise I felt a certain emotion. It was as if some hidden truth were being revealed before my very eyes. It was as if the group were finding their way not just to the soul of the dance but to something far beyond. It was a moment of revelation.

But there was one further stage as the individuality of the dancers began to re-emerge. This time, creative innovation and flair was a manifestation of the collective will, of the living thing which is the dance, and not an expression of ego. Each individual dancer had their own style, or *way*, their flourish or elan, but now this was elevated to become an expression of the collective being of the group. The dance came alive, as in football the game comes alive. When the individual player is first and foremost a member of the team, then the whole team's play comes alive in and through that player's unique talent and vice versa.

*

Dance and football are not unrelated, they share many of the same skills and muscle groups. The *War Dance* is common to many cultures: the Native American war dance, the Zulu war dance, the Scottish Sword Dance, The Maori Haka, etc. These disciplines embody military skills, stories, myths and other cultural material, and are transmitted through repeated patterns, and practised again and again till they become automatic. These ritual forms are useful in multiple ways, not just for training and ceremonial purposes, but also in preparing for battle, focusing collective identity and will, and improving agility, stamina and speed – most of which are applicable to football.

There has been some discussion of Pele's relationship to the dance/martial arts form *Capoeira*, brought to Brazil by African slaves in the centuries after 1500.[12] Capoeira and other African cultural forms such as Samba, became socially acceptable during the dictatorship of Vargas in the 1930s, at about the same time that football was raised to a level of national importance. In the daily life of the black

Brazilian player, the two disciplines would have been virtually inseparable.

A combination of song, dance, music and martial art, its combative actions unfold to the rhythm of the one-stringed berimbau. Whether performed or not by individual footballers, it was a cultural form with which every player of African descent would have been completely familiar.

It is easy to see how Capoeira could be a factor in Brazil's footballing success. It gives shape to the rhythm, timing and creative innovation of the Brazilian game, providing a shared *way*, with its associated ethos and understanding, to each player. The narrative sequence of actions (or *kata* in martial arts – see Chapter 6) provides training in terms of balance, posture, intricate footwork, fooling opponents and creating new moves, all of which are essential to football.

Something of the inspired, astonishing play we have often witnessed from Brazilian players over the years can, then, be traced all the way back to its roots in slavery, and even to the African dance traditions that preceded it. Capoeira's unifying potential is enormous, generating a common awareness of one's teammates and what each is doing or intending to do. If a player's footballing instincts have been structured by the Capoeira discipline, then individual expression is manifest through these shared, common forms.

In general, the more closely a team shares a common discipline or set of practices, then the more forcefully each individual player's talents will shine forth in team play.

4
PRESSING

Our style was based on pressing the ball wherever it was … So even if the opposition right back had the ball deep in his own half, we still pressed him. We played high-tempo football, which meant we had to be extremely fit. When the score's 0–0 and there are three or four minutes to go, what do players do? They get the ball forward. My view is that players then are going looking for the ball. But if they can do that in the last few minutes, why can't they do that from the start?

Graham Taylor [13]

The attacking team logic must apply not only to attack but also to defence. If the team works as a single unit, then attackers will play a supporting role in the defence.

Pressing, when the opposing team has possession, is a job for both defenders and attackers. It can be applied in an offensive position high up the pitch, in the midfield, or in a defensive position. But to be effective it must also be a team effort, in formation, performed with a single will. It must be fast, intuitive, with all players working together to close down the spaces that are needed by the other team in order to be successful in attack.

Barcelona are particularly adept at applying this principle. They apparently have a *six-second rule* whereby they seek to regain possession within this time frame by crowding the opposing player with the ball, while the rest of the team move to retain formation.

Constant pressing, done properly, will result in mistakes by the opposition, opening cracks in their teamwork, creating an imbalance which, once possession is regained, can quickly be exploited in a counter-attack. Indeed, the whole objective of pressing is to gain possession so that an immediate attack can follow.

We believe in striking quickly from defence … A team is most vulnerable when it has just failed in attack. If I had to suggest an ideal number of passes I would say three.

Alf Ramsey [14]

The martial arts form *Krav Maga* embodies a forward-moving, physically committed momentum. One interesting aspect of *Krav Maga* is the simultaneous combination of defensive and counter-attacking moves. Similarly, in fencing, the whole orientation and execution of the parry is designed as a launch for the counter-attacking riposte.

In football, the speed of transition from defensive to offensive movements is vital. They must be inseparable, without pause, and completely spontaneous. The defensive movement is a springboard for instantaneous attack. Catching the opposing team off balance naturally gives an enormous advantage to the attacking team. This crucial moment of transition should be the focus of intense team practice. It should be the signal for an explosive attack in which the whole team works as one. It should harness the maximum kinetic force available to the team when working together like a catapult, so there is a fast transition from potential to kinetic energy, with the ball riding the crest of the wave of attackers towards the opposing goal.

In pressing, we see the crucial importance of the position and movement of players off the ball (i.e. the other players not challenging for the ball). A whole team pressing at high speed takes the initiative and forces errors. For example, by pushing play to the flanks it can improve its numerical advantage in certain areas of the pitch, it can close down the passing lanes of its opponents, and open space behind the opponents' defence for their own attackers to exploit.

But this system can only work if each player has a complete understanding of what the whole team is trying to do. When, for example, an attacker presses the opposing defender near his goal, he must know intuitively that his midfielder behind will cover him by positioning himself to close down that defender's passing opportunities. The attacker does not have time to look behind to check before committing himself to the tackle; the team must press and strike as one.

For whole-team play, *zonal marking* is preferable to *man marking*. It means the defender is not fixated on a single opposing player, but more conscious of play in general, the positions of other players, and spaces opening and being closed off. Zonal marking goes hand-in-hand with this necessary whole-team awareness, which means a common feel for how each teammate will respond to play. And it is this unity which provides the basis for coordinated whole-team pressing.

A team under enormous pressure of attack is more likely to forget its training, lose formation, and revert to instinct or perhaps even panic. So it is essential that it has completely internalised its defensive strategy so that its instinct is to play in this way under extreme duress. Again, the endless practice of the appropriate training ritual is the key.

When we beat Brazil in the 1998 World Cup they played 35 per cent of their passes forwards and we had 65 per cent, and I made the statement that if they had played 65 per cent of their passes forwards we wouldn't have stood a chance.

Egil Olsen on the Norway vs. Brazil game.[15]

From the opposite perspective where the opponents defend doggedly by pressing, the solution is not to concentrate on retaining possession, but to move forward more aggressively, running into space more quickly, passing more quickly and so stretching their defence until cracks finally begin to appear.

It is very frustrating to see a team that is in possession moving forward, and, even though the defending team is perhaps off balance, then slow down and begin to pass the ball backwards, returning it eventually to their own keeper. Whether a result of laziness or simply an attempt to retain possession, this kind of play is depressing to watch. In the face of a hard-pressing team, trying to retain possession is counterproductive and, in the end, the more risky option, since a costly mistake will eventually be made. Adventurous, creative and risky attacking play is more productive than the so-called low-risk passing typical of possession football.

A team that makes forward momentum the fabric of its *being* cannot play slow possession football without disrupting its equilibrium. *It will always attempt to find forward-moving solutions to a pressing defence, to play and run into empty space and again to 'be' the team it is.*

5
SINGLE TEAM, SINGLE WILL

They were really an amazing side ... They'd get into threes and fours without really knowing they were doing it. They were playing 'habit football' after a time, and habit football was star football. They could find each other by instinct. They'd have a rhythm; go from the left side of the field to the right but make progress of 30 or 40 or 50 yards as well. Keeping the ball all the time. You have to have a lot of skill to do that, and we trained all the time on it.

Vic Buckingham on his Ajax side.[16]

Survival for the ancient hoplite Greek warrior lay in teamwork: in the phalanx where he stood side by side with his fellow soldiers.[17] The coordinated and well-rehearsed tactics of the Greek citizen militia stood in contrast to the more traditional warfare, which had been dominated by the heroic duelling of the aristocratic elite. The pragmatic nature of the

Greek system meant they could prevail against larger forces and more talented individual fighters.

In Homer's *Iliad*, Nestor speaks to his troops before a battle:

> *Now don't get over-confident, any of you,*
> *Or be too eager to fight the Trojans alone,*
> *In front of the rest. But no falling back either.*
> *Either course will weaken the line.*[18]

In the transition from the English *dribbling game* to the Scottish *passing game* in the 1870s we might see a parallel. The more muscular dribbling game, which focused on individual players' skill and audacity, had evolved out of the English public school system. The Scottish passing game on the other hand, with its proletarian origins, displayed a more group-orientated ethos and proved to be more effective tactically.

The Romans later further developed the phalanx tactic of the Greeks, and the Roman Empire was the result. The Romans, the Greeks, and the teams of the passing game alike, were all less interested in drama and glory, and more pragmatically focused on the defeat of their opponents.

*

There is an interesting relationship between the single-willed team-play which we want to pursue here and the concept of *Total Football* invented by the Dutch in the 1970s, whose prime mover was Rinus Michels, manager at Ajax.

Michels had played under the Englishman Jack Reynolds, who was manager of Ajax in the 1940s and before. Reynolds believed passionately in attacking, offensive football, an approach adopted wholeheartedly by Michels. The attacking *pass-and-move* system is all about the dynamic use of space: creating space, and moving into space. The importance of the concept of space in Dutch culture and consciousness[19] meant that Dutch footballers were particularly perceptive to thinking this way about the pitch.

Though there were many factors which fed into the emergence of Total Football, this idea of space appears to be central. The other crucial cultural idea, that of *totality*, first appeared in architectural theory in Holland in the early 20th century, and re-emerged in the 1970s. It means understanding the mutually dependent relationship between a part and the whole of a system, and further, that the parts of a system can be interchangeable.

The basic idea of Total Football is that each player has the ability to play in any other position. This flexibility and interchangeability is a powerful tactical weapon. But training and playing in such a way has an equally powerful effect on team coherence. It means that each player develops a whole-team understanding. Each player develops a feel for what every other player is doing, anticipating their intentions and so making fast, spontaneous play a reality. It also means a heightened awareness of space and movement as play unfolds, with less psychological distraction. It furthermore means a better use of *off the ball* movement. Combined with their attacking approach and aggressive pressing, it made Ajax almost unbeatable at their height.

One game that influenced the development of Total Football was Celtic's attacking victory over Internazionale in the 1967 European Cup Final, especially the use of attackers in defensive positions: 'Celtic fans knew that they had a chance because the team didn't play like everybody else. The backs – Jim Craig and big "Tam" Gemmell – were actually forwards, which had never been seen before. They were up beside the wingers Jimmy Johnstone and Bobby Lennox every game. Whenever Gemmell or Craig got the ball they were at liberty to go up the pitch and that baffled other teams because they couldn't work out how these guys got the freedom on the park.' Jackie Connor.[20]

The Hungary team of the 1950s (The Mighty Magyars) also had an influence on the formation of Total Football. Their star attacker, Ferenc Puskas, commented, 'When we attacked, everyone attacked, and in defence it was the same. We were the prototype for Total Football.' Like Celtic, all of whose players came from within 30 miles of the club, and many of whom had trained together as youths, the core of the Hungarian team had trained together at their club side, Budapest Honvéd, ensuring a unified style.

Uniformity of technical skills across the team is a further reason why Total Football was so successful: it adds a further level of team unity and understanding, through the collective rituals of training. Its front–back mobility and the use of overlapping defenders also means a coordinated relationship between defence and attack, with seamless transitions allowing instant forward movement.

Outstanding individual talent expressed through such a strong common team *will* is then elevated to stratospheric heights. In the case of Ajax, the presence of Johan Cruyff meant that the Ajax of that time was not just a great team but would also be a legendary one.

Twenty years earlier Scotland had its own Cruyff figure, in the form of Gordon Smith. According to the Daily Record's chief football writer *Waverley*, he was 'the most artistic, the most accomplished, the most graceful footballer in Scotland … he proceeded to shoot from almost every conceivable angle, with either foot, and from all sorts of distances ... he could twist and turn, sway and swerve and beat two, three opponents ...'.[21]

Hibernian's 2–3–5 formation was already considered passé by the time of their phenomenally successful period at the end of the 1940s and beginning of the 50s. But formation and playing-system are two quite different things. Apparently the *Famous Five* attackers (Laurie Reilly, Bobby Johnstone, Willie Ormond, Eddy Turnbull, and Gordon Smith) would constantly switch positions during a game and so confuse the opposition. Rangers forward Willie Thornton described them as: 'like a swarm of wasps, the way they buzz around you, interchanging at will.'

Robert Dunnett in *Picture Post* (March 19th 1955) described their attacking style: 'Hibs were playing a quicksilver kind of football ... Smith playing right wing collects the ball in midfield, whips it to Ormond on the left touch-line and begins running full speed up the middle of the field. Ormond holds the ball only for a few seconds, then puts it precisely where he knows Smith has arrived and that is the equaliser. Other teams try such a manoeuvre occasionally. Hibs keep trying it for ninety minutes.'

Hibernian toured Brazil in 1953 and drew with their national champions, Vasco da Gama, at the Maracanã stadium. They seem to have impressed their hosts so much that the Brazilian *Encyclopedia of Football Tactics*, published (before the World Cup) in 1970, included a whole chapter on the methods of Hibernian's *Famous Five*. Hence there is an argument that their unique playing system had a significant influence on the Brazilian style.[22]

Hibernian's success was due, not just to their mastery of the basic skills, but to their ability to internalize their playing system so that the relationship between their players was completely intuitive. With each player being fully attuned to each other's ways and talents, their uncanny abilities were feared by the opposition. Like the Dutch, their ability to switch playing positions resulted in a style of play which was creative, unpredictable and constantly evolving through new permutations.

In the *Total* system, interchangeability means much more player manoeuvrability. It multiplies and expands the triangular patterns of passing, so play becomes completely unpredictable to the opposing defence. More creative freedom opens up the structure of space on the pitch. It opens up new spatial possibilities, meaning in practice a greater variety of triangular combinations, and so a proliferation of routes to goal. It adds another dimension of attacking creativity to the playing system.

They ran and passed the ball in strange, beguiling ways, and flowed in exquisite, intricate, mesmerising patterns around the pitch.

David Winner [23]

Training is designed to permit a fast flow of the ball through this constantly changing triangular network of passes. Ball control, fast reactions, perfect timing and an intuitive feel for the spaces opening up through forward runs, are some of the crucial skills honed through endless practice.

... there was almost a kind of telekinesis. [Cruyff] seemed to know where everybody would be in the next three seconds. Not only was he kicking a ball in a certain direction, he was also making sure his player would appear in that place at exactly the right time.

Dirk Sijmons [24]

The more completely internalised the team system becomes through training, and the more the team shares the same instinct, then the more scope there is for creative intuitive play, and the less need for thought.

People couldn't see that sometimes we just did things automatically. It comes from playing a long time together. Football is best when it's instinctive, when it comes from the heart …
We didn't realise that the ball was going that fast, that we were changing positions so much.

Barry Hulshoff [25]

The argument for simplicity is strong: the simpler the system, the more easily the team *becomes* that system. Bill Shankly once said: 'Football is a simple game based on the giving and taking of passes, of controlling the ball and of making yourself available to receive a pass. It is terribly simple.'

*

In the *Total* system there is a dynamic relationship between the part and the whole which is constantly renewed. The player finds meaning in relation to the team, and vice versa. There is no fixed relationship between player and team, but instead an ongoing process of readjustment.

The *Total* idea, then, is cyclical, like the cyclical nature of *being*. The relation between player and team system must be constantly renewed. This ongoing process requires the momentum to be maintained through the repeated ritual of training, i.e. endless repetition with innovative variation. It is a process which deepens and matures over time. As player's abilities develop, they can explore new possibilities in play.

This cyclical process is also true for attacking play in general. Consistently good play requires the perpetuation of this momentum, so that the individual–team relationship maintains its vital creativity. It is a bit like a plate spinning on a stick. Without the added momentum it will fall, but if the spinning motion is maintained through the right training regime, play will continue to be imaginative and fresh.

It is in effect a positive feedback system: the more a team attacks, the more practice it gets in solving defensive problems and developing skills, the more creative its play becomes. In other words, the more a team attacks, the better it gets. The aim should be to establish and perpetuate the momentum of this cycle both in training and in play.

It is the momentum of this cyclical ongoing process which generates and maintains single-team *will*, like a lens focusing light to a single point. Any great team will lose its edge if this focusing process falters – it must be continuous, constantly renewed through established and endlessly repeated training rituals.

If the regime changes, perhaps players or the manager leaves, or there is a shift in emphasis towards defence or possession football, then there will be a lapse in the momentum of this cycle. That living thing which unites and binds the members of the team turns to dust, and so a marked decline in performance will follow.

Van Gaal's recent struggle at Manchester United, for example, might be a case of this kind of failure of momentum. His team lacked the fast intuitive play displayed so well by his incredibly successful Ajax team of the 1990s. The system can become sterile and pedestrian without the kind of intense team training required to create a simple team-wide intuition. A resurgence of thought and ego means the loss of a team's vital intuitive spark.

Modern coaches are too tactically involved. Too much systems ... They think too much about this simple game. The talent of the players is decisive: one should play naturally. No thinking, please! No thinking!

Jan Mulder [26]

Intuitive team play is a product of training well, but not usually seen as an aim in itself. Its crucial importance is often missed. When there is a fall in performance other explanations are found, but for the most part it is simply because the team has lost this ability to play as one.

However, even the greatest team in the world is in danger from psychological factors. It may play with a single, iron will, but if only one player starts to think too much, then the whole team's play will suffer.

We may forge a single team *being*, a team which acts as one, through the intensive repetition of team rituals, but impediments to this unity will occur as a result of both circumstance and human nature. A solution must therefore be found to neutralize and remove these impediments. Most of these obstacles dwell in the realm of the psychological.

Lack of motivation, for instance, should never be a problem for a team that makes attacking play central to its *way* of being. Strong motivation would be that team's default mode, because it is not a psychological state; rather, it is integral to the team's very fabric.

If a team is fully in the moment, at one with play, completely engaged as a single *team being*, and the play flows intuitively without hesitation, then we can say this team is in a state of authenticity, in Heidegger's sense. In this state, the psychological is tuned out of the focus of consciousness, and disengaged. Confidence is a natural aspect of this state. Again, it is not psychological, but a state of competent 'doing', characterized by a kind of ease and joy. As the psychological is absent, there is no question of fear or doubt.

If a player or players lose focus and slip back into the psychological and begin to think, then all those negative obstacles to this ideal state of play may reappear. The recent World Cup game between Germany and Brazil (2014) is an example of what happens when the confidence of one team soars, and they play even more intuitively, and the other team collapses as they think too much. As the German team took the lead they relaxed, played with greater ease, confidence and spontaneity. The further this process continued, the further ahead they went. The Brazilian team, on the other hand, began to fumble and make more and more mistakes as they panicked, became overwhelmed by doubt and completely lost confidence. Their team unity and discipline was replaced by individual thoughts of failure, humiliation and shame. Their team was finally reduced to eleven isolated, disjointed individuals.

Patriotic fervour in a team, while laudable, only serves in the end to undermine performance. The Scottish national team, for example, has a tendency to follow a particular narrative arc in a game, starting with wild optimism and ending in heroic defeat. A manager's first priority should be to dispel such a mindset. The psychology of individual effort inspired by patriotism breaks the unity of team focus and will. Individual emotion may greatly motivate individual performance, but individual heroism is not sufficient against a competent adversary; it is team play that wins a game. To be successful, national teams must leave behind external pressures and beliefs, keep cool heads and a pragmatic, professional attitude, and remain totally focused on play.

Likewise, frantic celebrations after scoring a goal become a distraction and ultimately disrupt team focus. The relief, and release of tension, which follow a goal leave a team fragmented and open to determined counter-attack. The celebrations are short-lived and soon appear hopelessly premature.

The ideal team maintains confidence and discipline at all times, even when several goals down, or facing defeat. It is, moreover, immune to psychological tricks, dirty play, poor refereeing decisions, etc. This is, firstly, because in training to be a team you cease (temporarily) to be an individual, and secondly, because you have trained (as part of the sequence of rituals) to ignore all the normal stimuli for individual thought. While normal players are subject to anger, fear, desire, egotism and self-consciousness, the player from the ideal team is not only fully engaged in the game, but also has a clear understanding and practical grasp of how *not* to think. Not-thinking is a learnt skill like any other.

To mention the word 'meditation' in a football context is to risk ridicule. Its association with a hippy or New Age mentality means that it appears the antithesis of a masculine sport like football. But it should be remembered that Zen meditation was practised by Samurai warriors and other martial artists in the East, many of whose lives depended upon becoming one with their sword, wielding it with total concentration.

Zen discipline is simple, direct, self-reliant, self-denying; its ascetic tendency goes well with the fighting spirit. The fighter is to be always single-minded with one object in view: to fight, looking neither backward nor sidewise. To go straight forward to crush the enemy is all that is necessary for him. He is therefore not encumbered in any possible way, be it physical, emotional, or intellectual.

D.T. Suzuki [27]

The common perception is that meditation is about passivity, but it is in fact the apotheosis of action. It is not a voyage through inner consciousness, but more like a cat watching a mouse: a complete, undiluted readiness for action. It involves a focusing of will until, like the point of a knife, it becomes a singularity. But it is not an individual or ego-based will, but a collective, shared or transcendent will: exactly the kind of will which the team, as one being, will wield.

The image of a football team sitting cross-legged, meditating, is one which would no doubt provoke a few laughs. However, there are many other practical drills and exercises which can be used to teach the same skills of total concentration and the negation of thought. In the end, the ability to resist thought during play means a greater toughness and resilience in a player, and even more so when shared by a team.

With individual egos disengaged, team training and team being can advance. Once psychological impediments are removed, play and transcendent will can flow as one. The point being that a great team in play has a totally different state of *being*, a state in which individual psychology has no place. The psychological concept of oneself must be relinquished temporarily as a kind of 'surrender' to the team. But that surrender brings with it an extraordinary new state of being. It then becomes clearer why great play, with the eclipse of individual ego, takes on a quasi-religious or spiritual dimension.

*

A single, unified team *will* is by far the most important factor in the pursuit of brilliant play. It allows an intuitive, spontaneous performance: a shared logic of doing, and shared creative improvisation, by all members of the team.

Constantly repeating a ritual structures the performer's instinct. A team that constantly performs a ritual together develops a shared instinct. In practice, a shared instinct means a shared spontaneous understanding about what needs to be done, and how to do it. It means a shared will.

The ritual, repeated till it can be performed automatically, is a narrative sequence of actions which gives shape to our will. So wherever we may be in that sequence, we have an instinct about what comes next. In a game of football played for real, our instinct is essentially our disposition to act in a particular way, to pass or move according to the positions and movements of teammates.

Because attacking play leaves no time to think or calculate, all actions must be determined by this instinct. The mechanism of attack demands shared spontaneous creativity, so the more deeply that instinct is shared by the team, the more decisive attacking team play will be.

The learnt ritual provides a shape for the never-ending flow of will. The team that plays with a single will is connected to the momentum of transcendent will (that irresistible urge to 'do' shared by all living things). The flow of the team's being in play then becomes one with the momentum and flow of Being itself. The team must not hinder or interrupt that flow, but instinctively feel that flow and allow it to drive its play forward in attack.

The momentum of transcendent will is also given form through the conventions and 'rules' of the game. Those rules are not simply a printed list of *dos and don'ts*, but a living thing embodied in the practice of the game itself: in every game that is played, in every player, in the pitch, each stadium, every football club, the ball itself, in the rituals of the fans, in the whole phenomenon of the game. It is the collective, global, *way* of football, and it is part of the *being* of the physical universe.

The conjunction of this flow of Will with the cultural structures of football, and in particular with the discipline of its attacking logic, is where the mystery and magic of the game reigns supreme.

6
NOTES ON TRAINING

I am a great believer in bringing in young players straight from school and indoctrinating them with the Spurs way of playing football ... We train the players to have only good habits. I tell them to treat the ball as their best friend and always to pass it with care and consideration. Belting the ball with an anywhere-will-do mentality has no place in the Tottenham way of doing things.

Peter McWilliam, 1925.[28]

Football is like a religion to me. I worship the ball, and I treat it like a god. Too many players think of a football as something to kick. They should be taught to caress it and to treat it like a precious gem.

Pele

Creating a great team is not a question of assembling a group of talented players, but about training, training, training. Rituals are not just what we do, they are what we *are*. These repeated structures of our *doing* are the foundation of our being, and this is true for both individuals and teams. So if rituals form, or change, us, at the most basic level, then the creation of a great team through training is all about rituals, and this is the most important point about team-building.

In the football world, rituals are usually known as drills. In fact the football world is awash with drills. Wherever we look, in books, training manuals or on the internet, endless training drills for teaching various tactics or skills are readily available.

I will argue here that a team should first concentrate on only a few basic drills, or rituals. What is essential is that these rituals be completely internalised so that they become spontaneous and automatic in play. They must be capable of being performed intuitively; only then do they become useful. In fact, they not only become useful, but provide the basis for truly creative and innovative play, the kind of inspired play worthy of a great team. Like jazz musicians, the song must be performed a thousand times before a transcendent interpretation becomes possible. Then the magic can begin.

It is not exposure to a variety of drills and rituals which is important, but depth of understanding and aptitude in performing those which *are* practised by the team. Half-learnt drills and partial exposure to numerous tactical systems will only confuse teams and hinder the fast intuitive flow of play we seek. Intellectual knowledge of the playing systems used by great teams of the past, or in other countries, is next to useless if those systems are not practised endlessly and completely absorbed and digested by the team as a whole.

*

The martial arts training sequence is known as *kata*. Like a ritual or drill, it consists of a series of linked movements and techniques intended to be practised until it can be performed automatically: 'By practicing in a repetitive manner, the fighter develops biomechanical responses that enable him or her to execute those techniques and movements in a natural reflex-like manner … The ultimate goal is to internalize the movements and techniques of each pre-arranged sequence (kata) so that they can be executed under almost any circumstance, without thought or hesitation.'[29]

The kata system is a product of the fighter's need for survival in the ancient military world. Technique is codified, systematised and arranged in the proper sequence to give form to the fighter's instincts so that in the heat of battle, under extreme stress, he can still perform in a professional and effective manner without being overwhelmed by fear or panic.

Once completely learnt, the kata, like the ritual, brings form and meaning to the user's world, to his or her very being. It embodies a particular way of seeing the world, with its accompanying values and emotional responses. The football drill, in a similar way, once completely internalised, structures the way a player *sees* the pitch and the flow of play. He sees that play as potential for action. He sees the game in terms of the opportunities it presents for *doing*, and these opportunities are determined by the internalised structures of his instinct.

Katas, like rituals and drills, can be performed either by individuals, groups or whole teams. The football kata or drill combines a sequence of moves designed for a specific situation. It may be for attacking, defence, for pressing, or any number of set pieces or circumstances. The attacking drill, for example, will determine the timing, rhythm, distance and direction of movement, all of which work together to penetrate the other team's defence. For whichever situation, the kata or drill is the route to intuitive performance and unconscious execution during the stress of play. Each and every drill is an opportunity for team-building, as it collectively structures team instinct.

A team must seek to do the basic things as well as possible because a rich creativity results from the complete mastery of just a few techniques. A limited number of internalised abilities provide a basis for unlimited creativity and innovation, for endless possibilities, uses and applications in play.

The repetition of the practice ritual is an iterative process, which means that each time the cycle is repeated the performers learn something new, and take a step closer to perfect play. As technical skill improves and the ability is internalised, more room opens up for creative innovation, which again leads to further technical prowess, and so on, driving the cycle forward. Because the practice ritual is a whole-team ritual, it is that joint creative innovation which gives form to the players' common instinct, their shared will, and so, also, to their shared being.

The momentum of this cycle of improvement follows the shape of being itself. But it is the creative impulse at the centre which provides the engine for the cycle – this is the crucial element in making human culture meaningful.

There is of course a deep gulf between practising a drill and using those skills for real in a proper competitive game. In creative play, we aim to transcend the ritual forms, not be bound by them. But their mastery provides the first step to a higher level of awareness and alertness on the pitch. In the end, team training aspires towards this quasi-religious dimension of single-willed creativity and artistry.

*

Behind this success was the drilling of Lobanovskyi and Zelentsov... Plays were meticulously choreographed and repeated over and over on the training ground until they became second nature. Defenders had to know how to attack. Attackers had to know how to defend. The switching of roles and inter-changing of positions was 'Total' and done without a second thought.

James Horncastle [30]

To recap, then: a great team has a single being, it plays with a single will, and flows like a force of nature, powerful, elegant, implacable. The way to transform a team into a single being is through the endless repetition of collective rituals. Not just any rituals, but those chosen to embody the football values and tactics we consider most important. Through practice the team must *become* the tactics, the playing structures and the attacking strategy.

Mastering the basic attacking and defensive movements is crucial, but if the forward-moving attacking dynamic is to be the most important aspect of the team, then rituals and drills which practise those moves — passing into space, diagonal runs forward, etc. — must be dominant in the training regime. They must not only be dominant, but practised until the endurance of the players is severely tested, until they are exhausted and never want to see another football again in their lives. Team being most firmly takes hold at the limits of endurance, where players are more likely to shed their individuality and find meaning in the common structures. Common rituals means common understanding, and at its optimum level this means collective singularity of will.

The primary attacking drills should not allow passing directly to another player, or passing backwards, except as part of the forward-moving attack. They should require constantly finding collective ways to shake off defenders, and especially to pass forward into space to meet a running teammate.

You used to have a stupid thing – well I thought it was stupid (at first) – where if you passed it and didn't move two or three yards you were penalized, and that soon taught you that you had to move.

Alan Hansen on training at Liverpool.[31]

Some drills will also involve pairs of players working on quick one-two moves, and trios or small groups on more complicated attacking structures. One-touch drills, repeated incessantly, bring shared rhythm and timing, and fast intuitive attack. If this is successful and these skills become second nature, then the team, to devastating effect, will embody what many regard as the true spirit of football: its creative attacking ethos. Furthermore, if that team's creative talent allows them to constantly innovate by switching playing positions, or even changing playing styles, then truly visionary football will be the result.

Some managers recognise the value of five-a-side play in training, as it helps players develop nearly all the crucial skills. It calls for rapid attacking play with fewer touches on the ball and a more focused use of teamwork. It demands a greater awareness of space, with fast movement off the ball to receive the next pass, and requires versatility in playing position. Extensive practice results in unhesitating spontaneity, honing of ball skills, and greater understanding of the use of space in the unfolding of attack.

If a player can master these skills in five-a-side, they have an advantage when they move back to the full-sized pitch, where their quick reactions can have a greater impact in the bigger spaces. Therefore it makes sense to develop attacking drills and rituals for the smaller, five-a-side format, which can then be practised endlessly to further focus a single team will.

... if there was any secret to Liverpool's success it lay in the fact that the fixation with five-a-sides gave us an extra edge on match days. Bigger pitches and goals made us feel we had more room.

John Barnes[32]

If attacking football is all about the use of space, then the smaller, five-a-side pitch only serves to magnify its importance. Play in a smaller space calls for faster reactions and more automatic, intuitive decision-making. It demands that players more consciously find space and move into space. It demands that players more deeply understand and explore its properties.

This deeper understanding means a team can more easily share a nuanced grasp of the pass-and-move system. The structure of that system becomes internalised collectively, binding the team as one, so that their play, constantly flowing, takes on the quality of music.

Shankly's Liverpool shared with Ajax this preoccupation with training endlessly in confined spaces: '[At Ajax] you had to play for your life and train for your life … Every morning we played 8-a-side in a very confined space (a small square), one touch, two touch … It was very high-powered stuff.'[33] Both teams focused on reducing reaction times: control, pass quickly and run into space; control and shoot. Razor-sharp and lightning-fast, these basic skills were constantly improved through rigorous repetition.

Ajax trained relentlessly in triangular formations to hone their rapid-fire passing and movement. 'We believed in repetition. Every day. Every day … we trained in triangles, passing and kicking in triangles, with very short control and a lot of movement between three players. From a fixed position this created a lot of possibilities. We trained endlessly, endlessly in small spaces.'

Gerard van der Lem[34]

For Liverpool, a series of shooting boards were arranged to create spaces for a variety of high-pressure close-quarter drills practising ball control. Players were required to be constantly on the move: 'The epitome of this was the 'sweat box' or 'shooting box'. The players worked in pairs in a square box surrounded by four shooting boards. One player would shoot and the other player would have to hit the rebound in his stride. It was like a four-way squash game and was very hard work.' [35]

Training 'never varies, week in, week out, the routine is exactly the same'.

Phil Neal [36]

Both clubs operated these intense, ritualised training systems to perpetuate the fast triangular structures of passing which constitute the attacking pass-and-move approach. It meant they could maintain the momentum of that cyclical process of focusing team *will* through shared instincts and common understanding, and so perpetuate excellent play week after week.

*

A further set of drills should be aimed at our second objective of developing the players' ability not to think during play. They will enable the team to resist the psychological and remain firmly present in the moment, fully focused on the play unfolding through and around them: remaining calm and focused, not only when things go wrong, such as when defensive mistakes or unfair refereeing decisions are made, but also, and especially, after their own side scores a goal.

Such drills and practice games could involve a variety of stressful scenarios where individual players and team alike can learn detachment and resilience when faced with things such as: certain defeat, verbal abuse, rough play, biased refereeing, cheating and other provocations. Similarly, over-confidence and arrogance are not only unprofessional but also impractical, since adverse events or failure can leave that player totally deflated or dispirited.

In training, Rinus Michels would sometimes create what he called 'sharp games' where the referee would deliberately favour one side or the other to stimulate adrenaline and focus concentration.

*

... at his first training-session, his first act was to teach his players how to tie their laces properly: 'Get the basics right,' he said, 'and the rest will follow.'

Fred Pentland, when he arrived as coach at
Athletic Club de Madrid, 1925.[37]

An even more radical approach would be to re-train a team in all aspects of physical play, as if they were children beginning the game. This means dismantling players' ball skills, habits, posture and movements and re-training them again from scratch, but this time collectively, as a team. In this way the logic of shared technique also becomes a means to shared team being.

In disciplines such as acting, singing and ballet, posture is the basis for all future learning. Correct posture is virtually a prerequisite for excellent performance. Many practitioners of these disciplines use Alexander Technique as a basis for correct body use. I remember in 2008 seeing a player run down the wing at a Chelsea vs. Arsenal game. He showed remarkable poise and ball skills, and I had the strong impression that his success as a footballer was in some part due to the excellence of his posture. His name was Samir Nasri.

Good posture is essential if the player is to develop their skills and realize their full potential. It is the touchstone of balance, speed, mobility and all the ball skills in his repertoire – passing, shooting, dribbling, volleying, trapping, heading, etc.

The Roman army drilled in minute detail, with several types of standing posture, foot movements, turns, marches at different paces, and ways of holding shield and weapons in particular positions according to the point in the drill. Every aspect of the army's movement was codified and controlled. These fundamentals not only provided a solid basis for more complex manoeuvres and strategies, but powerfully unified that army into a single fighting force with an unbreakable will.

Breaking training down into the smallest possible units forms a solid basis for the understanding and development of bodily skills. The articulation (or clear separation) of parts is not only vital for intellectual understanding, but also for physical, muscular and intuitive understanding. It allows the development of gesture and movement unimpeded by bad habits, tension and muscular spasm, which would otherwise limit that development.

Disciplines such as music, language-learning and football all depend on narrative flow and rhythm in the unfolding sequence of play. And so clarity of understanding and the articulation of parts is essential for the future creative juxtaposition of those parts, for improvisation and innovation where necessary. And since all those individual skills and techniques are learnt collectively, then that creative innovation in play becomes possible for the team as a whole; the team as a single being.

Fitness, moreover, is absolutely essential for the kind of attacking and pressing football we wish to play. And again, whatever method of fitness training programme is chosen, that regime can provide a further opportunity for strengthening group cohesion and cooperation.

Though ritualised practice is at the centre of the training programme, there must also be recognition of the role of classroom study. For example, the analysis of opposing team formations and playing systems, and the formulation of counter-strategies, is a necessary part of the preparation for each game.

All tactics should be thoroughly explained before being internalised through endless practice. Intellectual understanding is a firm basis for practical understanding. Firstly, grasping what the team is trying to achieve is a crucial prerequisite for intuitive skilled performance, but individual players have different strengths and weaknesses. Some learn better aurally, others visually, or through following demonstrations. Therefore a flexibility and openness towards teaching methods allows each player to fulfil their potential.

Moreover, the importance of discipline and professionalism in the training arena should not be underestimated. There should be no disruption of the collective learning experience, and the bullying of teammates should not be tolerated, as it is toxic to team unity. For success, the club must create the right environment for training, one which demands rigour, seriousness, and mutual respect.

Successful clubs place much emphasis on a training system for local youth talent, developing their skills at an early age. Barcelona's Cantera is a good example, with many of their most successful players following this route. Four of Hibernian's *Famous Five* forwards were local youngsters who came through the club's own training system.

Where youths come through such a system year by year, learning in the same style, team cohesion and shared playing come naturally. A coherent team *way* means a shared will. Moreover, within such a system, young players can learn multiple skills, allowing them to play in various positions and giving them the universality of skills so important to the modern game.

This is a strong argument for having the club firmly rooted in its own heartland, true to its tradition and fans. It is another level of authenticity, in both the conventional and in Heidegger's sense. It means a shift away from celebrity players and expensive transfers to the development of home-grown talent.

Perhaps there is a mood now amongst fans for a return to more authenticity in this sense. When a small team does well through hard work with local players, sometimes with a whole team costing less than a single player from a bigger club, there is a much stronger emotional reaction.

The relationship between a club and its heartland should be something like that between a wine and its landscape: a sincere embodiment of its heritage, tradition, territory and local culture. Even the most cynical fan would acknowledge that such teams are somehow more true to the game than those which result from a huge budget.

*

The most important factor in the Beatles' success, other than their individual talents, was their time in Hamburg. Over 16 months they performed their songs around the clock. This endless practice resulted in a totally unique group *being*, where their collective will meant a profound understanding of each other and the tools and materials of their creative trade. It meant that for a time their very different personalities were transcended by an almost unbreakable group dynamic, and resulted in eight years of unparalleled, constantly evolving creativity.

... the Beatles were in no respect an ordinary phenomenon. Many have spoken of the charismatic atmosphere that switched on whenever all four were together – a group-mindedness which kept them united ... They displayed ... at their peak a mutual understanding and collective intuition which kept them acutely in tune with each other and their time. The heart of the Beatles was an x-factor, a near telepathic connectedness ...

Ian MacDonald [38]

The performance of a song is essentially the performance of a ritual. It is a narrative sequence with a specific order over time, and with the space for creative expression or improvisation. A song, like any other ritual, performed many, many times, has the same effect of generating a joint instinct in its performers.

Twins often give the impression of a telepathic connection. They may simultaneously think or do the same things, apparently without direct communication. This connection can largely be explained using the concept of ritual, without any reference to their shared genetic origin.

From the very beginning of their lives twins share the same mother–child rituals, feeding and changing rituals, play rituals, the same rituals of interaction with other family members. As they get older the twins learn to be individual agents together. They learn to *do* through the same rituals of socialisation and education. Their *will* is structured in the same way; they share the same instinct. They learn to see and understand the world through the same eyes. It is not so surprising, then, that they have an uncanny similarity in the exercise of that will, in their activities, preferences, in their *way* in general.

Similarly, in football, it is training, through the endless repetition and complete mastery of a select number of ball skills and specific tactical rituals, which gives a team the ability to play with a single will, and, like the Beatles, to innovate, play joyfully and find their way to creative inspiration in each and every game.

7

THE COACH

The coach is the team's focal point, so preparing the tactical formation is essential. Every player must know where he has to be and support his teammates. There has to be absolute discipline and mutual understanding. Discipline is the basis of creativity and flexibility.

Louis van Gaal [39]

Great teams are usually associated with great coaches: men (until now) of vision, discipline and understanding. They have the uncanny ability to get the best from their players while using strategy and tactics in new and imaginative ways. Perhaps, more importantly, they have the ability to inspire their players to make a commitment to the team rather than to their own self-interest. They seem able to instil a sense of destiny and ambition in their team.

The list of great coaches would be much too long to include here (see Jonathan Wilson's *Inverting the Pyramid* for a sense of the coaching diversity and depth of talent the history of the game has witnessed, and, interestingly, the influences and interconnections between them), but managers such as Brian Clough, Bill Shankly, Rinus Michels and Jock Stein have a number of important things in common.

Each has an uncompromising singular vision, and the authority and self-belief required to implement that vision. Each has a firm commitment to the work ethic and attention to detail, sometimes to an obsessive degree. They are all deeply emotional characters who demand loyalty, dedication, professionalism and seriousness. The basic idea seems to be, do the simple things well, so well in fact that we could do them in our sleep, so that when they become automatic, they provide the basis of pure football.

The force of these figures' personality gives them the authority to impose the necessary discipline and rigour – a team *rule of law*. 'Football is war', according to Rinus Michels. Clough 'drilled his players in systemic intricacies and psychological toughness ... unrivalled at the time'.[40] Allied to this strict discipline is a strong value system: attacking play must be performed with honesty and fairness otherwise winning means little. Passion and emotion are likewise key parts of the ethos. Every one of these interconnected elements is vital to overall success.

We did it by playing football; pure, beautiful, inventive football. There was not a negative thought in our heads.

Jock Stein on winning the 1967 European Cup.

I want good, clean, attractive football.

Brian Clough's character in the film *Dammed United* (2009).

Each of these managers has a shrewd understanding of psychology. They choose their players carefully, knowing by instinct who can become team players, and how each can be motivated and encouraged. They dominate their players psychologically and refuse to let ego disrupt the whole-team focus and awareness. Michels described how, when he arrived at Barcelona, the players had a tendency to retreat inwards mentally when playing badly, and how, with Cruyff's help, he turned this habit around.

I don't need a boring book by [Sigmund] Freud to show me how to [read people]. I've been doing it since day one in management. I can tell, from the moment I see someone in the dressing room, whether he's off colour, had a row with his missus, kicked the cat or just doesn't fancy it that particular day. I know who needs to have his arse kicked. I know who needs leaving alone to get on with it … It's a special kind of coaching done only by very, very good managers – like me. The art of management is knowing your own players, and I'm not talking about whether someone has a better right foot than left. I'm talking about really knowing them, knowing what sort of person you've got on your hands … and I don't remember Freud winning a European Cup final.

Brian Clough

Each of these managers has an iron will, and is able to make his team manifest that will in play. Whether we describe that will as belonging to the manager or not is a semantic question; the crucial point is that the team *plays* with a single will. Their teams – Nottingham Forest, Liverpool, Ajax and Celtic – all played with that crucial single will, where self-belief and clarity of purpose in attack were central to what they were.

In play, team and manager share that single will, as they share the same rituals – they share the same team *being*.

… a man who is a manager and his players are honest with him and he's honest with them, he can transmit his thoughts to

them, and I'm certain I've headed some balls that were going into the net and I've kept them out and I've scored a few goals as well so that I've willed somebody to do something and they've done it.

Bill Shankly [41]

There are many similarities between Shankly's approach at Liverpool and Michels's at Ajax. As already mentioned, they shared a belief in attacking football, discipline, team ethos, excellent ball skills, and the triangular pass-and-move system combined with creative individuality. But is this enough to explain their success? Why did they get it so right?

Shankly seemed to have an instinctive understanding of what I call the momentum of being, the flowing transcendent will, or the physical joy of play – which he describes as 'natural enthusiasm' – and the knowledge that this force in his players must be uninhibited. It must be structured but allowed to flow freely with total belief and commitment, hence his complete faith in the simple, but fundamental, pass-and-move approach.

It is this pass-and-move system, combined with the creativity of individual players, whether Cruyff, Keegan or Toshack, which becomes both the Liverpool Way and the Ajax style.

Anfield's emphasis was on passing the ball and keeping the moves simple. Players fitted into the Liverpool way while giving it an added dimension.

John Barnes [42]

Right from the time he arrived at Liverpool, Shankly had a clear idea about what he wanted to achieve: 'Shankly is a disciple of the game as played by the Continentals. The man out of possession, he believes, is just as important as the man with the ball at his feet … [he] will aim at incisive forward moves by which Continentals streak through a defence when it is "closed up" by British standards. He will make his players learn to kill a ball and move it all in the same action ... he will make them practice complete mastery of the ball.' *Liverpool Echo*, December 14th 1959.

This description contains the two principal elements in both Shankly's and Michels's success. But it is the way these two things combine in a devastating mix, which is key. First, for both of these teams the skilful, triangular pass-and-move structure is always moving forward in attack. The frame of reference is advancing. The team retains possession, but while moving forward towards goal. Play is constantly flowing, but with a creative dimension.

And secondly there is a relentless and obsessive passion for doing the simple things well, a vigilance towards the basics and an attention to detail. This requires a high level of intensity in training, with tasks constantly repeated until their repetition becomes ritualised. Both managers understood that great play requires an unceasing cyclical process of constantly repeating the fundamentals of play. That the momentum of this cycle must be maintained at all costs.

If I had a job to do, even if it was scrubbing the floor, I wanted my floor to be cleaner than yours ... If everybody does the small jobs to the best of their ability, then the world would be better, and football would be better, so what we want is hard work, and no football club has ever been successful without hard work.

Bill Shankly [43]

A thorough intuitive grasp of the basic skills means this simple passing system can make complex, unpredictable patterns. These great teams showed an intuitive understanding, a clear sense of how play will unfold across time in the development of the attack. That four-dimensional understanding became a part of each team's very *being*.

Before I had the ball I knew exactly what I would do with it. I always knew two or three moves ahead … If ball control comes naturally to a player, he needs only one touch to get it where it needs to be. This is not the case if a player in possession has to stop and think. A pass which is a fraction of a second too late will have repercussions in the pass after that, and so on … You have to give the ball at the right moment … If I get the ball, the third man can run immediately.

Arnold Muhren [44]

Expressed as a simple mathematical equation, we might get: *obsessive attention to basic skills + attacking passing structure = exciting flowing creative play*

It is in the moment of full-team attack where all division is transcended. All division between players, and between players and the world, is erased, and only the single team *will* remains. This is the moment of revelation, with its quasi-religious resonance, which Shankly and Michels so successfully invoked time after time, in game after game.

*

Each of these managers share an intrinsic understanding of the importance of ritual within their regime, and its central role in delivering training systems, meaning and values, indeed all that is important in their 'way' of managing. Those rituals provide the stable structures, the solid ground necessary for a team to flourish and grow.

All of these managers are united in their belief in pure attacking football. It is the touchstone for all that is meaningful in the game. Football without attacking lacks a heart. They understand that though the defence is largely reactive and so relatively lacking in creativity, the attack is proactive, so that its forward momentum, like music, speaks to the human spirit. Attacking is the essence of the game because it is inseparable from artistry, beauty and creativity.

It may sound needlessly macho, but history bears it out – nearly all successful managers are determined to do things their way. Few succeed at trying to keep everyone happy or worry about what people think of them.

Scott Murray [45]

Great coaches will promote and defend the team ethos aggressively, attacking anything or anyone who threatens it. There can be no room for democracy here, but the dictatorship of the coach will normally be tempered by fairness and respect towards players outside the team context, since the team depends upon the commitment of everyone involved.

I maintain that a team is above all an idea … and more than an idea it is a commitment, and more than a commitment it is the clear convictions that a coach must transmit to his players to defend that idea.

César Luis Menotti [46]

These coaches become the father figure of their team family, a combination of boss, counsellor and therapist. They determine the team's way of life, what it feels, thinks, and most importantly how it plays. They are like the conductor of an ensemble. They set the rhythm and timing, raise the group awareness, get the detail right and choose the overall approach and strategy towards what they will play that day, whether a piece of music or an opposing team.

*

The four managers I have chosen here serve to illustrate in practical terms the principles advocated in this book: that a disciplined structure of ritualised attacking practice combined with hard work will deliver, firstly, instinctive skills and abilities which are then the basis of creative play, and secondly, that the team's *being* will become focused so it plays with a single, decisive will, not disrupted by individual egos or underhand attempts at gaining an advantage. Together this means speed, commitment and fast unhindered attacking performance, with artistry, skill and creative flair.

Obviously, the manager does not need to be an intellectual, but they require an excellent practical understanding of football culture, clear communication, and a grasp of human psychology. Their success depends upon the extent to which they can ritualise their singular vision through thoroughness of execution, and create the circumstances to generate that all-important singular team will.

All great coaches have a sense of the transcendent. Through great play they reach to something beyond. But one coach is worthy of special attention. Marcelo Bielsa, manager of Argentina, Chile, etc., has been hugely influential to the modern game. Obsessive, determined and driven, he emphasizes whole-team pressing, and then, when in possession, creative attacking moves.

In music, repenitización is used for the practice of playing a piece without having practised it first. The term in football clearly has some sense of improvisation while also carrying a sense of urgency. It sums up the counterintuitive idealism of the Bielsa philosophy, demanding that players repeatedly do things for the first time, a paradox that perhaps suggests the glorious futility of what he is trying to achieve. 'The possible is already done,' Bielsa said during his time at Newell's. 'We are doing the impossible.' … Bielsa seems as interested in reaching for the absolute as in winning matches – and that, of course, gives him his cultish appeal.

Jonathan Wilson, *El Loco: The Obsessive Genius of Marcelo Bielsa.*[47]

This sounds similar to the philosopher and historian of religion Mircea Eliade, describing the ritual enactment of a creation myth. The ritual is repeated, but because it re-enacts the creation, which is a unique event, the enactment itself is unique. Its sacred dimension means it stands outside time, and though in one sense it has been performed again and again, it is still the one and only time of its performance.

Everybody, whether they were veterans or novices, played every game like it was the last of their career.

Sergei Aleinikov on Dinamo Minsk.[48]

The Japanese Tea Ceremony has a saying: 'First tea, only tea' *(ichi-go, ichi-e).* It means that this performance of the ceremony is unique, stands alone, and that those taking part live only in the present moment and give themselves to it totally.

Great football can be like that, by our becoming one with the play, the ball and with the team: we become one with will itself, beyond everyday time, and enter the realm where the miraculous is truly possible.

8
CONCLUSION

Great football is like a song, or a wave on the ocean: it flows, gathers and crashes forward. It has a magical quality. The spectator feels this transcendent quality and recognizes it as something true also to the yearning of their own being. Their experience of deep meaning is not a result of intellectual understanding or thinking; but because they too share that will (it also flows in them), they become part of the profound unity which is woven by the movement of that transcendent will, through the team and through the game. The flow of play, the team's will, and the team's being are all mysterious aspects of this one unfolding thing.

There are two crucial factors in the creation of a great team: first, the rituals of their training, which give structure to the team's will and determine its dynamic being as forward moving across time and space; and secondly, the ability to resist thought. The freedom from thought allows the free flow of will, of rapid, bold and uninhibited kinetic action.

Rituals, practised endlessly, lead to skilled 'doing' or skilled play, which is a particular way of *being* in the world. This is creative, intuitive, spontaneous and flowing; it is structured but unhindered, and it is the state which Heidegger called *authenticity*. Interconnectedness is a result of that unhindered flow of will. In this state, team members have an instinctive understanding of each other, of each other's purpose, which is their common will. Their connectedness is a result of their shared *being*.

As a single *being* the team *becomes* the attack itself. In that attack, each player's natural creativity is expressed through the team's shared instinct. So the team as one can then improvise, innovate, play unpredictably, in unexpected and surprising ways that are unbelievable, not only to the audience, but also to the players themselves. This, then, is the dazzling, explosive alchemy that every coach and every football fan desires.

Beyond the touchline there is nothing.

Jacques Derrida

Gordon Smith by Robert Dickson ca. 1950

... he proceeded to shoot from almost every conceivable angle, with either foot, and from all sorts of distances.

EPILOGUE

Many years later, while greenkeeper at North Berwick, my father, on cold winter mornings, would exchange greetings and occasionally reminisce with the hero of his youth. Gordon Smith, now in his twilight years, like some retired Homeric warrior, would find peace in solitary rounds of golf on his favourite links.

He remained however, the same remarkable, elusive player, with the same balance, poise and pace, but now in the golf swing: *The arc of the ball, an echo of a cross from the wing into the box, becomes an inner journey across space. And in each shot he again becomes the flight of the ball itself until every white line and boundary and face in the crowd is erased.*

Theory

- Great teams play as one, with a single will, as a single *being*.
- Great teams play fast, creative, instinctive, spontaneous, attacking football.
- They have a singularity and clarity of purpose in dynamic attack and in defence.
- Great teams have a complete grasp of the simple things, and this is the basis for their creativity.
- Outstanding individual talent is expressed through team structure, leading to inspired play.
- At their best, a great team's artistry has a sense of other-worldliness or mystical one-ness.
- *Being*, both for individuals and teams, is equivalent to the repeated structures of their *will*, of their action or 'doing'.
- The structures of will are cyclical, constantly repeated, constantly moving forward.
- These structures, which we call rituals, are not just what we are, but also the means of creating or changing what we are (our *being*).
- Shared team rituals mean shared instincts, shared understanding, and a shared logic of 'doing' in play.
- So we can create a unified team *being* through team rituals.
- And we can create an attacking team *being* through attacking team rituals.
- We can utilise the flow and momentum of *Being* itself, in play: in spontaneous attacking play, the team's *being* is at one with that flow and momentum.

Method

Much of the following might be obvious to trainers and managers, but extra emphasis on key points can make a huge difference to team performance. It raises the team to the crucial threshold beyond which brilliant play becomes possible.

- Create a disciplined, serious environment for training, with professionalism, a strong work ethic, meticulous attention to detail, and positive values.
- Distinguish *thinking* from *doing* – keep them separate.
- Intellectual understanding of tactics and method is not enough for good play – they must be internalised through practice; they must become automatic.
- Begin with simple classroom explanations of tactics and what training rituals aim to achieve.
- Set much of the training in reduced or confined spaces such as a five-a-side pitch or in an enclosed space like Liverpool's 'sweat box' (see p. 80).

Rituals or Drills

Establish a small number of drills, but they must be practised constantly, endlessly, until completely spontaneous and automatic for all players. This is how we generate a single team *being*, so it can play with a single decisive will.

Primary Drills:

1. Whole-team attacking rituals: passing into space on the run, one-touch play, one-two combinations, finding fast, forward-moving solutions to a tough defence.

2. Whole-team defensive drills.
3. Whole-team pressing drills.
4. Rituals of concentration, not-thinking, resistance to distraction and provocation.

Secondary Drills:

5. Ball skill rituals – skills broken down to smallest parts (including posture) and re-learnt from scratch; shared skills strengthen shared team understanding.
6. Drills practising transition from defence to attack.
7. Fitness training – team rituals as further opportunities for creating collective team will.
8. Youth training system: practise all of the above rituals.
9. Club rituals outside training sessions: eating, travelling, other team activities and events – ritualise these where possible. Also daily, weekly, match-day activities, etc.

The Aim

In the moment of full-team attack all division is transcended. All division between players, and between players and the world, is erased and only single team will remains. This is the moment of revelation towards which every player and every fan is aligned.

Notes

1 Dave Bowler, *Winning Isn't Everything: A Biography of Sir Alf Ramsey*, Gollancz, 1998.

2 Martin Heidegger, *Being and Time*, Trans. Macquarrie and Robinson, Blackwell, 1962.

3 Arthur Schopenhauer, *The World as Will and Representation (Die Welt als Wille und Vorstellung)*. First published 1818.

4 Alfred Polgar, journalist and intellectual of the Vienna coffee houses, 1873–1955.

5 Stephen Jay Gould, *The Brain of Brawn*, New York Times, 2000.

6 As, for example, in the works of Meister Eckhart.

7 See: R. May, *Heidegger's Hidden Sources: East-Asian Influences on his Work,* Routledge, 1996, and Graham Parkes (ed.), *Heidegger and Asian Thought*, University of Hawaii Press, 1987.

8 Arnav Bose, *The Zeitgeist of Schalker Kreisel – Blue Revolution in Germany.* See: thehardtackle.com.

9 Valeriy Lobanovskyi, Soviet-Ukrainian football manager, 1939–2002. See: uddhamsotto.com

10 Michael Caley, *The Washington Post.* April 29th, 2016

11 Egil Olsen, Norwegian football manager, b.1942. Interviewed in *The Blizzard: The Football Quarterly*, Issue 3, 2014.

12 Simon Kuper, *Football Against the Enemy*, Orion, 1994.

13 Graham Taylor, manager of Watford and later England, b. 1944.

14 Roger Hutchinson, *'66: The Inside Story of England's 1966 World Cup Triumph*, Mainstream, 2002.

15 Interview with Lars Silvertsen ('The Mind Has Mountains') in *The Blizzard: The Football Quarterly*, Issue 3, 2014.

16 David Winner, *Brilliant Orange, The Neurotic Genius of Dutch Football,* Bloomsbury, 2001.

17 Michael Rosenbaum, *Kata and the Transmission of Knowledge in Traditional Martial Arts,* YMAA, 2004.

18 Homer, *The Iliad,* trans. Lombardo. Hackett, 1997.

19 David Winner, *Brilliant Orange: The Neurotic Genius of Dutch Football,* Bloomsbury, 2000.

20 From Chris Hunt, *Local Heroes: The Lisbon Lions,* 2007. See: chrishunt.biz.

21 Willie 'Waverley' Gallagher, *Daily Record,* January 3rd, 1951.

22 Colin Leslie, 'Why Pele Has the Hibees to Thank!', *Daily Mail,* August, 1997.

23 David Winner, p. 2.

24 David Winner, p. 59.

25 David Winner, p. 40.

26 David Winner, p. 143.

27 D. T. Suzuki, *Zen and Japanese Culture,* MJF Books, 1959, p. 62.

28 Peter McWilliam, manager of Tottenham.

29 Michael Rosenbaum, *Kata and the Transmission of Knowledge in Traditional Martial Arts,* YMAA, 2004.

30 James Horncastle, *The Man Who Revolutionised Football.* See: espnfc.com.

31 Alan Hansen in Taylor, R. and Ward, A. and Williams, J., *Kicking and Screaming: An Oral History of Football in England,* Robson, 1995, p. 286.

32 John Barnes, *John Barnes: The Autobiography, Headline,* 1999.

33 Jan Molby, *Jan The Man: From Anfield to Vetch Field,* Gollancz, 1999.

34 David Winner, p. 232.

35 Andrew Ward and John Williams, 'Bill Shankly and Liverpool', in *Passing Rhythms,* Berg, 2001, p. 62.

36 Phil Neal, *Life At The Kop,* Queen Anne Press, 1986.

37 Jonathan Wilson, *The Guardian,* May 14th, 2009. (The club became Atlético Madrid in 1941 on the orders of Franco.)

38 Ian MacDonald, *Revolution in the Head: The Beatles' Records and the Sixties.* Pimlico Press, 1995.

39 Louis van Gaal, *The Guardian,* 16th May 2010.

40 Chris Mann, equaliserblog.wordpress.com

41 Bill Shankly, from the documentary *Shankly: The Legend.*

42 John Barnes, *John Barnes: The Autobiography,* Headline, 1999.

43 Bill Shankly, from the documentary *Shankly: The Legend.*

44 David Winner, p. 136.

45 Scott Murray, *Football for Dummies,* Wiley, 2010, p. 30.

46 César Luis Menotti (Argentine coach), see: totalbarca.com

47 *Eight By Eight,* Issue 4, February 2015.

48 Sergei Aleinikov (Russian player and coach, b. 1961). Sergei Aleinikov and D.I. Belenky, *I Zhizn, I Slyozy, I Futbol,* Polymya, 1992.

Bibliography

Aleinikov, Sergei, and Belenky, D.I. *I Zhizn, I Slyozy, I Futbol.* Polymya, 1992.

Bell, Catherine. *Ritual Theory, Ritual Practice.* Oxford University Press, 1992.

Bowler, Dave. *Winning Isn't Everything: A Biography of Sir Alf Ramsey.* Gollancz, 1998.

Certeau, Michel de, and Giard, Luce. *The Practice of Everyday Life.* University of Minnesota Press, 1998.

Davis, Bret W. *Heidegger And The Will, On the Way to Gelassenheit.* Northwestern University Press, 2007.

Dreyfus, Hubert L. *Being-in-the-World, A Commentary on Heidegger's Being and Time*, Division I. MIT Press, 1991.

Eliade, Mircea. *The Sacred and the Profane, The Nature of Religion.* Harcourt Brace, 1959.

Grayson, Edward. *Corinthians and Cricketers.* Sportsman's Book Club, 1957.

Handler, Andrew. *From Goals to Guns: The Golden Age of Football in Hungary 1950–56.* Columbia University Press, 1994.

Heidegger, Martin. *Being and Time.* Trans. Macquarrie and Robinson, Blackwell, 1962.

Herrigel, Eugen. *Zen in the Art of Archery.* Penguin, 2004.

Horak, Roman, and Maderthaner, Wolfgang. 'A Culture of Urban Cosmopolitanism: Uridil and Sindelar as Viennese Coffee-House Heroes', in Holt, Mangan and Lanfranchi. *European Heroes,* Routledge, 1996.

Kerr, Fergus. *Theology After Wittgenstein.* Blackwell, 1986.

Kuper, Simon. *Football Against the Enemy*, Orion, 1994.

Larson, Øyvind. 'Charles Reep: A Major Influence on British and

Norwegian Football', in *Soccer and Society*, 2, 3, Autumn 2001, 58–78.
Magee, Brian. *Wagner and Philosophy,* Penguin, 2000.
May, Reinhard. *Heidegger's Hidden Sources.* Routledge, 1996.
Parkes, Graham (ed.). *Heidegger and Asian Thought.* University of Hawaii Press, 1987.
Reep, Charles and Benjamin, Bernard. 'Skill and Chance in Association Football', *Journal of the Royal Statistical Society*, Series A, 131, 581–585, 1968.
Rosenbaum, Michael. *Kata and the Transmission of Knowledge In Traditional Martial Arts.* YMAA Publication Centre, 2004.
Schopenhauer, Arthur. *The World as Will and Representation (Die Welt als Wille und Vorstellung).* First published 1818.
Shaughnessy, James D. (ed.). *The Roots of Ritual.* Eerdmans, 1973.
Suzuki, D.T. *The Zen Doctrine of No-Mind.* Rider, 1949.
Suzuki, D.T. *Zen and Japanese Culture*, MJF Books, 1959.
Tolle, Eckhart. *The Power of Now.* Hodder & Stoughton, 2001.
Varley, Paul, and Isao, Kumakura. *Tea in Japan, Essays on the History of Chanoyu.* University of Hawaii Press, 1989.
Waley, Arthur. *The Way and its Power, A Study of the Tao Te Ching and its Place in Chinese Thought.* Grove Press, 1958.
Wilson, Jonathan. *Inverting the Pyramid: The History of Football Tactics*, Orion, 2013.
Wilson, Jonathan. *Nobody Ever Says Thank You: A Biography of Brian Clough*, Orion, 2011.
Wilson, Jonathan. *The Anatomy of England: A History in Ten Matches*, Orion, 2011.
Winner, David. *Brilliant Orange: The Neurotic Genius of Dutch Football.* Bloomsbury, 2000.

Index

The author, half-time at Craven Cottage.

Steve Dickson B.A. (Hons.), M.A., originally from Edinburgh, is a London bookseller and author of books on applied philosophy.

Contact

If you have any comments or questions please get in a touch at:
www.stevedicksonauthor.com or
www.adamandevebooks.com

Published by Adam & Eve Books, 2016

Available soon

GOLF AND THE RIVER OF WILL

The *Way* in the Cult of Golf

The search for great play is also a search for authentic *being*. In the singular act of the authentic shot, the line between self and world is revealed as a fiction, and the flight of the ball across space delivers an aura of deep meaning.

The impulse to 'hit' the ball is a cause of internal division and poor play. The answer lies in finding an 'external' will in the club, so player and club become one in the momentum of its flow. With a natural release from the top of the swing and a straight left arm, the downswing starts automatically, allowing correct uncoiling, timing and power. We see this transcendent quality clearly in the miraculous swing of Bobby Jones: not the act of one man, but the soul of golf itself.

THE DIET FIX

Weight-Loss, Cooking Ritual and the Authentic *Way* of Food

Weight-loss is incredibly difficult. But the answer is to forget dieting and give-up weight-loss. They are dangerous aims, only adding fuel and momentum to the vicious cycles which lie at the root of the problem.

Rituals of food determine our *being*. So first we must focus on those foods which dramatically affect our eating habits, rituals and cycles, i.e. sugars and other refined carbs.

Refined carbs undermine our being as free agents, they hijack the natural hunger cycle and enslave us. These inauthentic food habits turn us into passive consumers rather than the active beings which represent our true nature. We must seek an authentic *way* of food, a way of cooking and eating, true to the extraordinary creatures we are.

19599813R00079

Printed in Great Britain
by Amazon